Mess on the Floor

Have you got your **Layar** app downloaded on your smartphone?

You have?

Right. Let's begin.

Tap the **Layar** app.

And point your smartphone at this page.

Now here comes Puss.

Tap on **Hear me speak.**

Now you can put your smartphone down and listen to Puss talking Gaelic as you turn the pages.

What is this?

Dè tha seo?

On the floor.

Could it be quiche?

No dè theirear ris?

Or what's it called?

An e ìm a th' ann?

Or some cream dropped down?

Is it butter?

It's kind of gooier

Agus buidhe.

And yellow.

Very tasty

Fìor bhlasta

If it's pasta.

12

Don't say it's stinky poo!

Càit a bheil an cù?!

Where's the dog?!

I don't like that.

Cha toil leam sin.

Straight in the bin!

What's this I see?

Ò thì!, ò thì!

Oh dear, oh dear!

18

Oh good heavens!

O mo chreach!

I'm under attack.

Come on, doggie, get in there!

Tha e gaisgeil. Chan eil eagal air.

He's brave. He's not afraid.

Stop! Stop!

Sguir dheth! Sguir dheth!

Get out the way!

Old Puss must flee!

Cuidich mi!

Help me!

But wait a minute!

Ach fuirich mionaid!

There's something which …

... I didn't see.

The problem's sitting up above.

An sin! An sin! An leanabh!

There! There! The baby!

Download the app which will let you play the audio on your smartphone or tablet. The app is called **Layar** and is a free download. To activate the audio file of the text in this book you tap the app and point the smartphone or tablet at page 2 of the book, as though you were taking a photo. Puss will be pleased to see you and will read the story to you, in both languages. Purrfect. You can also download the mp3 file from our website at www.lexusforlanguages.co.uk

Gaelic consultant: Steaphan MacRisnidh
Gaelic voice: Mairi Iseabail Weir

British Library Cataloguing in Publication Data.
A catalogue record for this book is available from the British Library.

ISBN: 9781904737360

published 2014 by **Lexus Ltd**
60 Brook Street, Glasgow G40 2AB

© Lexus Ltd, 2014

www.lexusforlanguages.co.uk

App feature thanks to Newnorth Print Ltd
Printed and bound in England by Newnorth Print Ltd